T0131652

THE
MASTER
KEY
Unlock the Mysteries
of the Kingdom
of Heaven

FEVEN GEBREYESUS

WESTBOW
PRESS®
A DIVISION OF THOMAS NELSON
& ZONDERVAN

This book is a work of non-fiction. Unless otherwise noted, the author and the publisher make no explicit guarantees as to the accuracy of the information contained in this book and in some cases, names of people and places have been altered to protect their privacy.

WestBow Press books may be ordered through booksellers or by contacting:

WestBow Press
A Division of Thomas Nelson & Zondervan
1663 Liberty Drive
Bloomington, IN 47403
www.westbowpress.com
844-714-3454

Because of the dynamic nature of the Internet, any web addresses or links contained in this book may have changed since publication and may no longer be valid. The views expressed in this work are solely those of the author and do not necessarily reflect the views of the publisher, and the publisher hereby disclaims any responsibility for them.

Any people depicted in stock imagery provided by Getty Images are models, and such images are being used for illustrative purposes only. Certain stock imagery © Getty Images.

Scripture quotations are taken from the New King James Version. Copyright © 1982 by Thomas Nelson, Inc. Used by permission. All rights reserved.

ISBN: 978-1-6642-9063-1 (sc)
ISBN: 978-1-6642-9064-8 (hc)
ISBN: 978-1-6642-9062-4 (e)

Library of Congress Control Number: 2023901674

Print information available on the last page.

WestBow Press rev. date: 02/28/2023

"My cup runs over"!

—Psalm 23:5

Contents

Preface

We all have heroes. They can be Bible heroes or people we know in our own lives and call heroes. We look up to them and admire them. But more than anything we want to be like them, so we ask about them or take time to research them. We study their lives to find out how they became what they are. We see extraordinary beings who are courageous, resilient, powerful, and agents of change. And we think, *What did they do that I didn't? What more do they know that I don't? What's their secret? Is this secret reserved for a few, or can anyone access it?* We keep on wondering, and we easily get discouraged when we see how accomplished they are. We compare ourselves to them. Sometimes we try hard to imitate them and do what they do.

But it is not easy to become someone you are not, is it? Truth be told, we don't have to be them. As Christians, we want to know God and be powerful witnesses to Him in everything we do. Most of us desire to make God known in our lives, but we don't know what to do or how to be. We see only the outcome and think it can't be done. Shedding tears in prayer, losing hope, doubting God, and a lot more become parts of our everyday lives. Fear not! God is for us. He sees our tears and suffering and comes to save us. He not only saved us so we could escape eternal damnation. But also continues to save us from our fears, burdens, insecurities, and doubts daily. He will show us which ways lead to victory and answered prayers. Listen! These people didn't become heroes overnight. They had their struggles too. How did they overcome them? That is the question we should be asking. The answer to our question is in the Bible. The Bible has recorded for us stories of different people from different walks of life who overcame because of God.

If you struggle with these issues, this is your day! This is God's visitation day! And the Lord said, "I have seen the oppression of my people who are in Egypt and have heard their cry because of their taskmasters, for I know their sorrows. So I have come down to deliver them out" (Exodus 3:7). Although He said this to the Israelites, it applies for us too. He has come to deliver you! It is exodus day for you! God will shine His light upon you. God is faithful. Trust Him! You will be set free. You will find the paths that lead to Him and know Him. Isaiah 55:12 says, "For you shall go out with joy, and be led out with peace." God's paths are filled with joy. He will not only show you what to do but also lead you with peace, and your life journey will be filled with joy.

Through this book, you will find the keys to knowing God more deeply and finding His ways so you will walk in them, honor Him, and become a hero in the kingdom of God. God will reveal Himself to you. Jesus said, "... the knowledge of the mysteries of the kingdom of heaven has been given to you" (Matthew 13:11). You are not the only one who desires to know Him. God wants you to know the truth too. That's why He has given you knowledge of the mysteries of heaven. The Lord is faithful. He is very near; call Him and He will answer you. The Lord wants to build a relationship with you. He is the one who loved you first. He is the one who is constantly calling you to come closer to Him. He is ready to reveal things to you. You will discover the mysteries of His kingdom. Through this book, I will show you how life as a born-again Christian can be so much more empowering and fulfilling than life without Christ. You are not alone in your Christian walk. Come to the word of God—the only and abundant source we have been given to guide and light our ways. You will see your life being transformed into the likeness of Christ. The Holy Spirit is our helper. I am a living testimony. God is truthful. If He says it is, then it is. If He says it can be done, it can be done. There is no doubt about it.

Introduction

Most human beings are curious about what is beyond the world we know. We would like to search for the unknown, to touch the unseen world and comprehend it. While some deny that an unseen world exists, most of us are convinced it does. So we search for it and try in many ways to learn more. It is intrinsic to our nature. We can't help it! It is the way we are created. But the whole world is going its own way. We have made our paths and rejected the only true way that was made for us. The one true way that we should find is God's, our creator's, way.

Any appliance or machine you can buy comes with a manual. In it is the purpose for which it was made and instructions on how to use it. The source of the manual for human beings is the inventor Himself. If you don't want to follow the instructions that are listed there, then you will suffer the consequences, possibly serious damage. The manual states what dangers could result if you don't follow the instructions.

In the same way, God created us. He is our source of the knowledge for what purpose we were made. He is the only and true way for which we should search and find so we know where we came from and, hence, where we are going. God has provided a manual to which we can refer. It is called the Bible! In it is information about who we are, what our past looks like, and what our future is going to be. Most of the prophecies in the Bible have come to pass, which makes it the most important book in the whole of human history. We can depend on it. The Bible tells us many things that concern us, like the fate of our world. But most of all, it tells us about God's plan of salvation through Christ Jesus our Lord and Savior. Jesus restored our relationship with the Father through the shedding of His blood. Now, thanks to Him, we can boldly enter the presence of our Father and enjoy our relationship with Him. It is God's delight to be with us, communicate with us, bless us, and reveal Himself to us. But it has to be a mutual agreement. God has given us the manual on how to find Him and His ways, but if we learn about Him and then decide not to accept Him, we cannot simply find Him. Likewise, after we accept Christ as our Savior, we must decide to follow Him. And this is so hard for most honest Christians to understand. They accept the Lord as their own Savior, they love the Lord, they go to church, and they do everything they can to honor Him. But they still don't understand who they are or who God is, and they don't have a personal relationship with God. They only know Him by hearing other Christians talk about their relationships with Him, and they wonder when that is going to happen for them. That is a sad reality!

Are you a Christian who has been staying in the house of the Lord for so long and yet has not shown much growth? Are you frustrated about why it has been this long? Do phrases like "You should have been a teacher by now" haunt you and make you feel inadequate? If you are feeling desperate because you don't know what to do about it, I have good news for you. God is for you and not against you! Your mourning days are over. The devil is a liar and often accuses us of using the word of God. The devil tested Jesus Himself with the word, not only once but many times. See, you are not alone. There is a way out! This way is Jesus. Today, you will find the way! Rejoice! Want to know how Jesus dealt with it? Here it is: Jesus dealt with the devil by quoting the right words from scripture. It is of paramount importance that we know how Jesus dealt with Satan because He is the author of our faith. In John 16:33, He tells us to "be of good cheer, because I have overcome the world." Through Him, we are already winners. For that to manifest, we need to know our Bible well. Just like our Lord Jesus, we need to study it. The Bible tells us in Luke 2:47 that Jesus was well versed in the scriptures by the time He was twelve, which astonished the teachers and everyone who heard Him. The secret lies in the scriptures! Jesus said to the Sadducees, "You are mistaken, not knowing the scriptures nor the power of God" (Matthew 22:29).

How often do you read the Bible? It is the very source for all the answers you need. I want to show you how to find God and your way in Him through His word. No more waiting! We are meant to live life to its fullest. Jesus said in John 10:10, "I have come that they may have life and that they may have it more abundantly." That is God's will for us. He wants us to enjoy life with Him! God knows your struggles; He wants you to know that He sees you. He won't let you suffer like that anymore. He wants you to know that He is the God of justice. If you are searching for Him and His ways, He will help you. Jeremiah 9:24 says, "But let the one who boasts boast about this: that they have the understanding to know me, that I am the Lord, who exercises kindness, justice, and righteousness on earth, for in these I delight, declares the Lord." He says it makes Him happy for you to know that He is a God of justice. If He says, "Search for me this way and you will find me," then you will find Him because He is truthful and just. What's more, He won't withhold anything from you. He is always ready to show you the way: "I will instruct you and teach you in the ways which you shall go: I will guide you with mine eye" (Psalm 32:8). You see that? He will teach you what to do, where to go, and show you the way. Rejoice! This is your day, the day that the Lord has made for you to receive answers!

The Bible tells us in Ephesians 4:11–13 that God gave the church teachers to edify it. Some are called to teach. These teachers help us understand the word of God, and as they explain, they make it simpler for us to understand. Thank God for such people! And although it is good for them to share from their knowledge, what we will learn is how God Himself teaches us by His Spirit. This does not mean that we will *all* be teachers. What it means is that we can learn from God and stand on our own instead of being dependent on others to teach us for the rest of our lives. We should stand on our own as well as share the gift with others in our Christian walk. However, this does not mean that, when God teaches us, we will walk alone. We are social beings into whom God put different gifts, so we serve one another and the rest of the world to fulfill our purpose. We learn from God daily to be empowered to live and serve for His glory. In the body of Christ, we are all interdependent, but we must learn to stand on our own before we benefit others. This book will focus on finding ways to stand on your two feet independently, equipped by God Himself. God will teach you!

So how does God teach you? He can teach you through prayer, circumstances, His creation, the testimony of others, and many other ways. In this book, we will discuss how the Holy Spirit teaches you through His word. You will see how the word of God plays a significant part in transforming our lives. The Bible is a mighty weapon in every believer's hand. And it doesn't cost us a dime! You could be wondering, *Well, who is going to bear with me and take the time to teach me?* The Lord will teach you personally. It is His delight to spend time with you. This is an opportunity for you to learn from God Himself, a one-on-one session with the Holy Spirit. "All your children shall be taught by the Lord, and great shall be the peace of your children" (Isaiah 54:13). God desires to spend time with you and teach you. He only asks you to give Him time. God is patient and not overbearing. He is not in a hurry to go anywhere. He has eternity! He is always willing to teach you.

In this book, we will be studying the word of God from the gospel of John, chapter 2, verses 1–11. This is a story in which Jesus and His disciples are invited to a wedding in a small town called Cana in Galilee. We are going to focus on what happened on that particular day, what we can learn from it, and if there is a pattern that we can use to replicate that same miracle in our lives today. There is a hidden but plain key to accomplishing a similar miracle in our lives that is far more important to us—manifesting the glory of God in our lives. You will see how the word of God plays a significant role in your Christian walk and be filled with the Holy Spirit, who is the agent of change. He will make His ways known to you. In Psalm 103:7, we read, "He made known His ways to Moses, His acts to the children of Israel." There was no man on earth in the Old Testament like Moses. God Himself testified for him, saying that He speaks to Moses face to face. This is the Moses who not only saw God's miracles but knew His ways. This is the Moses who did many great miracles of God. He heard directly from the Lord and wrote the first five books of the Old Testament. We can see that God can reveal His ways to whomever is willing to know Him better. You might be thinking, *I am not Moses, and there is no way I will ever measure up to him.* The good news is that you don't have to measure up to anyone but Christ. You are called to look like Christ. And Christ has already paid the price for you, so you can get close to God and access everything you want as His child. Yes, being under the new covenant is a privilege. You are required to do only one thing—just draw near to Him, and He will draw near to you. How? That's what I want to show you in this book: the word! That's it. Nothing matters more to God than His word, because His word is His personality! The Bible puts so much emphasis on the word that Psalm 138:2 says, "For you have magnified your word more than your name." The name of Jesus is the most powerful weapon in heaven, on earth, and in the sea. Can you imagine the word being more honored than the name? In Luke 16:17, Jesus says, "It is easier for heaven and earth to pass away than for one title of the law to fail." It is that important!

We will look at the chapter verse by verse because there are steps to be taken. Following these steps will make a huge difference in your life. It is important to understand that one step follows another for you to experience this miracle. The Holy Spirit is going to help you understand this, so with no further ado, let's dive in.

If you seek me with all your heart, you will find me!

— JEREMIAH 29:13

PART ONE

How to Be Filled by the Spirit through the Word of God

In the gospel of John 2:1–11 is a story about how Jesus turned water into wine in Cana of Galilee. This, records the Bible, was the beginning of the signs that Jesus did and manifested His glory, and His disciples believed in Him. It was just a wedding, nothing out of the ordinary. But Jesus chose to reveal Himself there. We often pray to God to reveal Himself to us and manifest His glory in us so others can see it and come to the light of God. We desire to be instrumental in God's hand to manifest His glory. That is a noble quest! But how do we do that? Why did Jesus choose to reveal Himself there? God uses many methods to reveal Himself to us, but today we will see how He uses His word to do that. We will see this chapter in depth, verse by verse, and God will help us understand.

8 ⎯ Your Body as a Tent

And on the third day there was a marriage. (John 2:1)

On an ordinary day during an ordinary ceremony, a miracle was about to happen to an ordinary family. Weddings have been held as long as humankind has existed, but what the Holy Spirit inspired John to record about this specific event is the unforgettable miracle performed by Jesus in front of many witnesses. Not only was it recorded as it happened thousands of years ago, but it also carries a lesson for us to learn today. Let's see how that applies to us in our times!

The kingdom of God is likened to a king who held a wedding feast for his son and invited many people, as recorded in Matthew 22:2–4: "The kingdom of heaven is like a certain king who arranged a marriage for his son, and sent out his servants to call those who were invited to the wedding." The parallelism between the verse in Matthew and the verse in John is that they both discuss weddings. The verse in John is about an earthly wedding, while the other verse in Matthew, which Jesus taught in a parable, is about a heavenly wedding. This is why we are going to apply this symbolism to this story. So let's set a foundational statement that the heavenly wedding has symbolic meaning in which God prepared a huge feast, an opportunity for humankind to live with Him and have eternal life through His Son, Jesus Christ. Taking this as an example, let's now consider the wedding at Cana of Galilee, to which people were invited. Likewise, each one of us is invited to the heavenly wedding by God the Father. But to get in we have to have an invitation card. We can get this invitation card only by confessing that we are sinners and accepting Jesus as our personal Savior and Lord in our hearts. Our hearts are in our bodies, temporary houses for us till we join in the heavenly feast for eternity.

Now consider our bodies as the wedding tent that is made for a temporary purpose. As we live our lives, people share in our happiness or sadness. Just like at the wedding at Cana, people come to share our happiness, achievements in life, and other events. We are social beings; we need one another. This is why we need to invite Jesus into our lives. We need Him more than anyone else. Through Him, we will gain access to eternal life and union with the Father, the Holy Spirit, and God's family. When we accept Jesus into our hearts, the Holy Spirit comes to reside with us. And when He comes, He is not like any other invitee. He will come to you regardless of who you are. God is no respecter of people. He shows up whether you are poor or rich. He shows up at your place, in your situation. You don't have to travel to meet Him. This is solely the mercy and goodness of God at work to pull us toward Him. When we come to Him and continue walking on His paths, we get to know who we are and what our purposes on this earth are. We all have access to this unfathomable pool from which we can draw strength, courage, hope, and supernatural power to fulfill what God has put in our heart of hearts—our inner beings. He is the one who helps us realize the dreams we have had for a long time, and He does this so He can reveal His salvation plan to all people through us.

8— Whom You Invite

Now both Jesus and His disciples were
invited to the wedding. (John 2:2)

We meet a lot of people in our everyday lives. Some of them remain strangers, and we don't even bother to remember who they are or what they look like. We become acquaintances with some. Others are casual acquaintances, while some are close friends. But a few of them become our dearest friends for life who share many happy and sad moments in our lives. These people get to know us deeply and know our likes and dislikes. We also know a lot about them. Although no one can know everything about others, we can say we know each other well enough. Our beliefs, interests, and lifestyles connect us. As the saying goes, "Birds of a feather flock together." By associating with people we bring into our lives, we either influence or get influenced. In my native language, there is a proverb that says, "Tell me who you go along with, and I will tell you who you are." This proverb illustrates that, whether you consider someone a friend or a foe, if you are constantly meeting up and conversing with them, you are already sharing their ideas, interests, and even standards and beliefs. The bottom line is that we look like the ones to whom we give the most of our time. If we give time to something good, we become good without much effort. And if we spend most of our time for nothing, then we become nothing. So when we give time to the word of God, we look like Christ—the Word. If we don't spend time with the word of God, it's no surprise when we look like the old, carnal human who cannot do the will of God. This applies to every one of us.

In this story, we see Jesus and His disciples at the wedding, having been invited to attend. We see Mary, the mother of Jesus, there too. It's probably a relative's wedding. Jesus has not yet performed any miracle publicly. Notice that the Bible considers our bodies as tents (temporary living) and our heavenly or transformed bodies as our forever and eternal homes. Second Corinthians 5:1 says, "For we know that if our earthly house, *this tent*, is destroyed, we have a building from God, a house not made with hands, eternal in the heavens" (emphasis added). Whenever I read this verse, I am immediately reminded of how Eritreans, my native family, hold a wedding ceremony.

Let me explain a few customs of my culture so you get the whole picture of what I am trying to say. Anyone who has a wedding to host borrows a big tent in which the guests enjoy the party. This tent is set outside the house of the host, mostly with the help of neighbors, some friends, and relatives. It is made to stand with iron poles tall enough to accommodate anyone who wants to jump for joy when they are dancing. It is made tall enough to release the heat trapped inside, too, because it can get really hot in there. It has only two openings: one is where the guests come in and go out, and the other opening is to the side and made to connect to the gate of the host's house. Long rectangular bars of wood are put on iron stools to hold them tight and serve as benches for all guests. The inside of the tent is decorated with fine linen or silk cloths of different colors to match the bridesmaids' and the groomsmen's clothes. Flowers are everywhere too. A separate table and set of chairs is prepared and decorated for the bride, groom, maids of honor, and groomsmen to sit. It is put on a higher level so that every guest can see them. It is a ceremony to celebrate the union of the bride and groom on one hand and their families on the other.

Posters taped to the walls of the tent say, "May the Lord make you like Abraham and Sarah." It is meant as a wish for a long and prosperous life that is blessed by God. Others say, "As we have seen you bloom like flowers, may we also see your fruit." This is a representation of the couple's marriage as a blooming flower and the children to come as fruits of the womb. After lunch, people dance, and then it is time for the bride and groom to cut the cake and throw confetti. As they leave, everyone comes out of the tent to bid them farewell. Most weddings are held in this manner. Every relative will come to attend a wedding, even from faraway villages. Every neighbor is invited to the wedding, not only to attend on the special day but also to participate in preparing the food and the traditional drinks and setting up and bringing down the tent after the ceremony finishes. Friends of the family are also invited. Even street beggars are encouraged to attend. It is considered godly to do charitable work and feed the hungry on the day of celebration. Some of the food and drinks also go to the church for the priests.

This day is a day for people to celebrate and share food with everyone, especially the needy. It is a noble culture. The expenses are covered by the parents of the bride and of the groom, but other relatives also contribute their fair share with anything they have, such as crops, sugar, oil, herds, or money. It is a communal effort that reflects the kind of life we have in Christ.

In a spiritual sense, the first time we understand the gospel and decide to accept the Lord Jesus in our hearts is the time we invite Him into our lives. This is like the wedding in Cana of Galilee to which Jesus was invited. It marks the beginning of our Christian life. Just as babies are born into this world, this is the time we are born again into the spiritual world, where we are expected to grow continuously—even though many people do not consider growth or strive to grow after they have made sure they are getting to heaven. They get stuck in the basics of Christianity and live their lives aimlessly.

Getting to heaven is the ultimate goal, but it is equally important to have a personal relationship with Jesus. It is the reason we are saved. The Bible says that Jesus will say to some people that He doesn't know them and that He will shut them off from heaven (Matthew 25:11). It is very important that you know that God saved you, so the relationship between you is like father and child. After being born again, you need to mature and know your place in the kingdom of God. Through this, you become a responsible Christian whom Jesus calls friend and coworker. You should be able to figure out for what you are here and what gifts you have so you can be of service to the kingdom of heaven and for the good of humanity. What God has put inside your heart is not for you; it is to help you serve others with your gift. You will find yourself growing in serving others. The Bible says in 1 Corinthians 12:12 that we are all parts of one body. Find out which part of the body of Christ you are and how you can use your gifts and talents for the greater good. But here is the thing: you cannot give what you don't have, or can you? It is possible to have the heart to serve others but also find yourself unsure of what to give and be at a loss on how to do that. When that happens, it could be discouraging. Do not fret! You are not alone. "Where there is a will, there is a way!"

You could be thinking, *I want that, and I have searched and prayed for it and asked people about it, but to no avail.* Let me tell you, today is the day that you will be transformed from seeking to finding and walking in the light of the truth. You will finally understand how things work together for those who love God. I want you to consider this: the Christian life is a lifelong journey of constantly seeking and finding. The ways of God are so deep. The more you seek, the more you will find—more knowledge, more wisdom, and more life. It is a lifelong quest. That makes it so much more interesting. As you continue walking in the light of the revealed word, you will find yourself growing and getting closer to God.

⚷— Enough Is Not Enough!

John 2:3–5

Basic knowledge about anything will get you started in that area, if not land you somewhere big. The wedding hosts thought they had enough of what it takes to serve others. But, in the story, we see that enough is not enough. Accepting or inviting Jesus into your heart and learning enough truth to support what you believe is right. However, as we keep on growing, this truth may not be enough for the battles we face in our everyday lives. The people hosting the wedding were not able to provide enough wine. Times like that make us wonder if we were right to follow in the steps of the cross because the burden of not knowing becomes unbearable and we suffer greatly. It makes us reconsider serving others when we don't have enough ourselves—and rightly so! We get confused and scared and feel lost.

But we don't have to be all of that. All we need to do is simply go to the feet of Jesus and learn from Him, just like Mary in the story of her and her sister of Martha in Luke 10:38–42. In the story, Jesus commended Mary and revealed an important truth to Martha, saying, "But one thing is needed, and Mary has chosen that good part, which will not be taken away from her." Yes, hearing the word from Jesus is the one thing that's needed from us. Spending time with the word is the one thing we need to change our lives for the better and find solutions to many of our problems. What's more, once you have read the word, it cannot be taken away from you. The word lives inside you! The word is Jesus Himself. He also said that, apart from Him, we can't do anything (John 15:4–5): "Abide in me, and I in you. As the branch cannot bear fruit of itself, unless it abides in the vine, neither can you, unless you abide in me. I am the vine; you are the branches … for without Me you can do nothing." If a branch is cut off from the vine, it falls down and eventually dries out. It cannot bear any fruit on its own. If you want to be full of life and bear much fruit for the glory of the Lord, then you must abide in the word. Otherwise, you cannot make it on your own. Desire alone won't get you what you are seeking. You want to preach the gospel with a demonstration of power. You know that what is recorded in the Bible stands true in your time as well. Perhaps you go out and try preaching but with no demonstration of power. You feel helpless. You understand that what you thought you had enough of is not enough at all. You want to know more. You know there is more to what you are experiencing. All you need to do is come to the word of God. The word itself is God. He has all the answers. He is an endless supply; abide in Him. *Abide* means to remain stable or fixed. Fix your eyes on Him—the word. Live according to His word consistently. The word is everything! Come to His word, and He will come to your level, teach you according to your pace, and lift you without being judgmental or demeaning. He is the best teacher there is!

We usually ask those around us for help, but sometimes they just can't, even if they want to. That is what was happening at the wedding. The wedding hosts must have shared their predicament with those closest to them, and Mary seems to have been one of those people. She went up to Jesus, the abundant source of everything, and told Him about the situation. In such a situation, it is obvious that the people in charge of the wedding are asking their loved ones for help and seeking a solution. But how could any of them be of help at that moment? But Mary knew whom to go to when things went wrong. She asked Jesus about it on their behalf. Does Jesus seem pleased with Mary's request? I don't think so. He only answered her, "Woman, what have I to do with you?" What does this mean? Was Jesus ignoring his mother, whom the Bible says He had obeyed all of His life? Luke 2:51 says, "Then He went down with them and came to Nazareth, was subject to them, but His mother kept all these things in her heart." There is a reason Jesus responded as He did. He was telling Mary that the people whom this issue concerned should come to Him directly and just ask. Likewise, He wants us to come to Him with all of our questions by ourselves and not go through others. He wants us to know that He is closer than our breath. He wants to communicate with us and have a personal relationship with each one of us. Jesus shows us that the way to go about it is to go directly to Him and ask Him. The wedding hosts had already invited Him and His disciples. They could have simply let Him know about the wedding. Perhaps their respecting Him as an honorable teacher made them feel ashamed of their shortcomings. They were trying to please Him and everybody else with what they had. Sometimes we try so hard to please God with our efforts, and we fall short. We don't remember that He is God and He knows how far our abilities go. God is waiting for us to come to Him and ask Him directly. It is for that very reason that the Father gave us His only begotten Son—to show us that He is much closer than we think and so much more understanding of what we need. Sometimes we think of Him as if He is watching us from a far, unreachable place and not saying anything or lending a hand when we fail. We often make a shrine for Him and treat Him like a stone God. This makes Him as good as any other idols; they have eyes but cannot see, have ears but can't hear, and have limbs but can't do anything or go anywhere. We forget that He is the one true God who sees, hears, talks, walks, touches, and does things for us. Our God is alive! He is able and mighty to save! Let's seek the truth directly from Him. The only way that we can help ourselves and others is by looking up to Jesus Himself. All that we have known, learned, and experienced, we ought to share.

Still, we should be careful about how we share the gospel. We need to be careful not to make people look to us when we share our stories because what we have is limited, but if we direct them to Jesus, who is limitless and the true source, they can get the help they need. Just like Mary, we sometimes take other people's matters into our own hands and plead with God to do something about the situation. Although He hadn't publicly done any miracles at the time of the wedding, Mary must have experienced at least a fair share of miracles as Jesus was living with her and her husband. Why else would she come and ask Him about it? By asking Jesus on behalf of the people, Mary served as an intermediary. Christ gave up His life to save us, paying dearly with His blood. He is the only intermediary between humans and God. But going through other intermediaries won't do us any good because God has given everyone who believes direct access through Jesus. This applies to everyone who has accepted Him under the new covenant. This era of mercy started at the time Jesus was crucified, died, and was raised from the dead.

The Bible says that God made us kings and priests: "But you are a chosen generation, a royal priesthood" (1 Peter 2:9). Let's consider our priestly privilege. What does a priest do? Priests have a relationship that enables them to represent themselves and others in the presence of God. There's no earthly priest that will represent you because Jesus made it possible for everyone who will accept Him to come directly to the Father God through His blood. You are a priest! God wants you to come into His presence represented by Jesus, the only one who is worthy to stand between you and God the Father. He wants the person in charge of the matter to come to him and ask. Why? Because He wants a relationship with each one of us; He wants to talk to you, teach you, heal you, and give you answers directly, not through some mediator. People can show you the way, but they cannot *be* the way. Jesus is the way to your freedom, to your healing, to your knowledge, to everything. Any situation you are facing calls on you to come closer to Jesus.

God wants you to come to Him and ask Him yourself, talk to Him, wait on Him, and seek Him about anything and everything. He is not your Savior and Lord for nothing. He wants to befriend you. He wants you to grow and to know Him well. Don't try to approach Him through people or special individuals you think are closer to Him. You can learn how they grew closer to Him, but never depend on anyone else for you personal relationship with God. God has given you the privilege of approaching Him yourself. You can learn from your friends, teachers, and mentors, but you can't depend on them all the time. That is not good for you. Others can tell you what works for them, but you will still need to find out what works for you. If you don't, you will get frustrated. And why should you when God is as close as can be to you? God is asking you to personally approach Him with your questions, confusion, feelings, and everything else. He is stretching His arms toward you, and His Spirit is ever calling you to get closer to Him. Come—your questions will be answered, your confusion cleared, your feelings acknowledged and healed. Who answers like God? No one! He won't shame you for thinking a certain way. He will gently teach you and lead you to the truth.

Look at what Mary did in the wedding story. She directs the servants to go to Jesus themselves. She was not offended that Jesus didn't give her the answer. It seems she understood that her role was to connect others to Him, the source. We see her changing her strategy. Not only did she motion them to go, but she also told them one foundational truth: They should do everything He asked them to do. This means that they were not to heed His words partially but should seek the whole truth. We tend to hold onto some of God's words and leave others. God gave us the guidelines for life in the His word. When we hold onto the whole truth, we understand better and live better. We are set free!

So that is why Mary told the servants to do everything He said without leaving anything out. The servants went and asked Jesus, and He told them precisely what they should do. Now, why did He do that? Because the issue concerned them directly; they were the once in charge of the water pots. They were the ones whose job it was to inform the wedding hosts whether they had enough wine or not. Imagine that you are given an assignment by someone who wants to hire you for your expertise. You have convinced them enough to be hired but end up falling short. You need to do something about it, but there is no time. What do you do? You ask for help! As these people in charge of the wine were seeking help, they came across Mary. She was an instrument in guiding them to the solution—Jesus. She told them what to do. They needed to go to Jesus themselves and do everything He told them to do. When we come to Him ourselves, He will answer us directly. Jesus said, "Come to me, all you who are heavy laden." He is an answer to anything and everything we need. Sometimes other people can't understand what you are going through, making you feel lonely and powerless. Come to Jesus! He understands what you are going through, and He will show you a way out or a way through. You will come out victorious. He will take your burden and lighten your weight. The Bible says in 1 Peter 5:7, "Cast all your care upon Him, for He cares for you."

He will set you free and strengthen you because He cares deeply for you. He is always waiting at the door of our hearts, knocking: "Behold I stand at the door and knock. If anyone hears My voice and opens the door, I will come in to him and dine with him, and he with Me" (Revelation 3:20). If only you would open for Him, you would be amazed at how His grace is sufficient to lift you even from the dirt, clean you, and cover you with clothes of glory. Psalm 139:8 says, "Even if I make my bed in Hell, you are there." You can never be too far away or too low for the grace of God to find you. So open this door to your heart. He will come in and dine with you. In this verse, *dine* means He will give you His unhurried time. He is available for you twenty-four seven. There's nothing you could tell Him that is too emotional or too insignificant. I dare you to try. He will guide you, counsel you, chat with you, and so much more. Whatever you ask of Him, He will do abundantly. He will be there for you whenever and wherever you need Him. Don't you want that? All of us want to know someone who is so dependable at all times, but that is an impossible task to ask of one another. We are only human. But God is God, right? He is able and faithful. Let's open the door to our hearts for Him. How do you open this door for Him? Let's see!

⌘⌐ The Symbolism of Water

When the servants came and asked Jesus what to do, He told them, "Fill the waterpots with water" (John 2:7). What does water have to do with wine? Often Jesus spoke in parables and symbols.

This is one of those times. Let's see what water symbolizes in the Bible. In Ephesians 5:26–27, water symbolizes the word of God: "that He might sanctify and cleanse it by the washing of water by the word." "Washing of water by the word" means the word is the washing agent, the water itself. When you ask God what you must do to be an instrument of glory in His hand, He tells you to simply be filled with water—the word. That's all that you need to do! Simple! Go and spend time with His word until you are full. If you want the Spirit to move in your life so that people see God's glory in you, then you need the word of God. And who is the word of God? It's Jesus Himself. "In the beginning was the word, and the word was with God, and the word was God" (John 1:1). "And the Word became flesh and dwelt among us, and we beheld His glory, the glory as the only begotten of the Father (which is the Son), full of grace and truth" (John 1:14, parentheses added). The "word became flesh" refers to Jesus, and Jesus is "the only begotten of the Father." Jesus was the visible revelation of the word of God. So whenever you come to the word, you meet with Jesus—God the son. Now that we have established that, let it be known that nothing happens if you don't honor the word, Jesus. The word of God says, "For the Holy Spirit was not given, because Jesus was not glorified" (John 7:39). It's true that the Holy Spirit cannot dwell in you unless you accept Jesus as your Savior. It is also true that, if you do not honor the word, you won't be able to see the moving of the Holy Spirit, let alone His glory. It also says in John 3:5, "You must be born of water and Spirit." The water is the word, and the Spirit is the Holy Spirit. The Spirit of God comes right after you hear the preaching of the word and believe.

All through the Bible, we see the Spirit of God at work.

Genesis 1:2 says, "And the Spirit of God was hovering over the face of the waters." You see? The water is the word, and where the word is, the Spirit comes to work miracles. Before God made the earth, the sea, and the heavens, first there were the waters. The Spirit of God always comes to glorify Christ the word—the waters. You get it, right? The Spirit moves whenever the waters are there.

Let's go back to the story in the gospel of John. Jesus told the servants to fill the waterpots of stone with water. Notice that it was not just one waterpot of stone; they were several. This leads us to ask why. John 7:38 says, "He who believes in me, as the scripture said, out of his heart will flow rivers of living water." This living water is Jesus Himself. When you are filled with the word and continue filling, then comes the overflow. Overflowing with the word means you have answers not only for yourself but also for others. You can now serve others. It is the living water, Jesus, who makes this possible. Wherever the rivers of the living water flow, they revive what was dead. They fill what was empty; they heal, deliver, and produce live things. Many pots in our lives should be filled with water—pots of the things that concern us and are a driving force in our lives. These are pots of belief, tradition, and philosophy. The Bible teaches us to guard our hearts most of all because all issues of life come out from them. We need to search and find out what the word of God says about these things and follow it as written. We need to change our thinking and our belief systems, according to the word of God. Only then are we following Jesus. Jesus said, "But why do you call me 'Lord, Lord,' and do not do the things which I say?" (Luke 6:46). Let what the word of God says is true be your truth! Just like Mary told the servants, do everything He tells you to do. Then you will see the pots of your family, ministry, career, health, and so on be filled and become as tasty as a good wine.

8⟶ How Filled Are You?

Jesus told the servants to fill the waterpots, and they filled them to the rims. He didn't say how much they should filling them; He just told them to fill them. God will tell you which way you should go, but He won't impose it on you. He will give you the opportunity to choose for yourself. How far you want to take it is totally up to you. Jesus said, "If anyone thirsts, let Him come to me and drink" (John 7:37). So are you desperate enough to go all the way until you find the truth? Then take a step toward that goal. Grab your Bible and read it. That's all it takes! How long will it take you to act on it? The servants just heard what Jesus said to do and did it immediately. Maybe they were in a more pressing situation, but how many times have you felt that you cannot lead anyone to Christ because you don't have the right answers yourself? You know you are on the right path, but telling it to others is a whole other challenge. Sometimes you feel so frustrated and tired of caving in when people confront you. When that happens, it's time to seriously commit to reading the Bible. It should be your priority if you want to courageously and joyfully share your faith and serve others.

People do all sorts of things when they are desperate. Whether it's for better or worse, they become decisive. There is nothing we can't do if we decide to take the initiative. When we first accept Jesus into our hearts, it's through a decision that we make to follow Him because we believe He is the way, the truth, and the life. Our decision to follow Him doesn't end there. It takes an everyday decision and commitment to follow Him. To do that, we just need to go to the only source we have—the Bible. Unless we are willing to search and find things about Him in the Bible, we will be led by the circumstances of everyday life. Deep inside us is a yearning to know Him and have a close relationship with Him, and that is possible only when we prioritize the word of God.

Suppose you meet someone on any given day and see real potential in this person to be a good friend or more and add value to your life. What do you do? You try everything to get to know them. You spend time with them. As time passes, your feelings grow deeper, and you might want to spend the rest of your life with that person. Again, you spend more time, and you constantly think about them. You start caring about things they care about. Why? Because now they are the most important person to you. What brought about all of this? *Time!* You give time whenever you think something is of value to you. You give time to what interests you.

Now, are you feeling that your spiritual life is not where it should be? Are you feeling there is more to your Christian life than what you have now? Then you need to decide to be committed to Christ, the Word of God. He won't disappoint you. You will find yourself where you need to be. Just give time on a daily basis, even if it is just a few minutes per day. You will realize that, after you start following through with your commitment, you will start loving it. You will end up giving it more of your time. Let me tell you, once you get there, spending time with the Holy Spirit teaching you, leading you, and guiding you through the Bible will be so exciting that it will become effortless. Why? Because you will fall in love with the Bible for teaching you who God is, for showing you who you are, for helping you determine what you believe, and for making you realize that someone up in heaven is tirelessly in love with you. He comes immediately when called; He will be there for you, carrying you through difficult times; and He never lets you down when you need Him. He will listen attentively to you and comfort you. So run into His arms. He is always trying to reach out to you—*even now!*

"Now is the accepted hour, now is the day of salvation!" (2 Corinthians 6:2) declares the word of God.

⑧— Test Time!

After the servants filled the pots, Jesus told them to draw out some of the water and take it to the master of the feast for testing.

When you are filled with the word, you are already filled with the Spirit, who quickens every good work in you. Why? Because the words that Jesus spoke are spirit and life, according to the gospel of John (6:63). That is the time that God starts to perform signs and miracles in your life. This is only the beginning! The Spirit of God is at work in your life for the better. He will first fill the void that you have in your heart, and your soul will be satisfied. "You have given me greater joy than those who have abundant harvests of grain and new wine" (Psalm 4:7). He will give your life meaning. You will experience the joy of the Lord that is beyond any knowledge. He will equip you for whatever challenges you face in life, and He will cause you to go out in victory and come back in victory. He will strengthen you so that you stand firm when it is test time. Let any expert come forth to test you—of the body of Christ, of the world, or of the devil. They can only marvel at how you can continue to be good till the end.

8— Tried and Found Good!

The master of the ceremony (the expert) called the bridegroom and said to him, "Every man at the beginning sets out the good wine, and when the guests have well drunk, then the inferior. You have kept the good wine until now" (John 2:10). Everyone wants to make a good first impression, but under the test of time, their true colors start showing. Let's face it—who can pretend every day of their lives and still get away with it? It is so tiresome! Of course, you will let your guard down once in a while, and when that happens, what you have been building for a long time—your reputation—can be destroyed. It's the strength we have been faking for people. It's the brave face that we have been putting on. It's the politeness that we have been pretending to feel. It's the ugly side of our evil nature that we have been working so hard to hide! All of it pops out in one way or another as time passes. And we often don't learn from our mistakes, trying to build on shaky ground once more. How long does it take for us to return to the Lord, ask for forgiveness, and get right with Him? If we come to Him, He will come to us. He will gladly embrace and build us up. Doesn't the Bible say, "Unless the Lord builds a house, they labor in vain who build it" (Psalm 127:1)? Let go of the pride! Let's lay our burden on Him who cares for us. He will instruct us and teach us His ways. He will enable us to walk the righteous path. And in due time, He will perfect us until people see Him in us.

The master of the wedding ceremony didn't know what had happened. He didn't know that Jesus was behind all of this, and he praises the bridegroom. When we give the word of God time and allow God to work in our lives, people will see excellence in what we do and in the way we live. They will see our uniqueness. They will marvel at how we can keep on being real and still good all the time, with no need to pretend. When we invite Jesus into our lives, He becomes abundance in our lack. When you are full of the word, Jesus, the Holy Spirit comes and transforms you. You become good all the time. With or without your knowledge, you display the character of God at all times, and God is good all the time. We are made in His image and His likeness "to be conformed to the image of His Son" (Romans 8:29). And you don't have to worry about making a good first impression on people. When you are filled to the rim with the word, you will be good the first time people meet you. You will remain good as time passes. You will be good at home, at work, wherever you go, and whenever it is. You will become as free as can be. No need to worry! Just be. Anyone and everyone will see God in you all the time, in your weakness and your strength. Yes, even in your weakness! The Bible says in 2 Corinthians 12:9, "My strength is made perfect in weakness." You see? No matter who you are or what your life's purpose is on this earth, with God you will know where you are headed and what your end is. He will give you light and understanding of how to fulfill your calling.

⚷— The Symbolism of Wine

God's glory is manifested in your life. The word of God ends this story by declaring, "This beginning of signs Jesus did in Cana of Galilee and manifested His glory; and His disciples believed in Him" (John 2:11). Yes! Signs and wonders will be the testimony of your life after you experience the fountain of life Himself. God will manifest His glory in you and, in return, honor you. Remember, the honor doesn't come from drinking water; it comes from a taste of the best wine! What is the symbolic importance of wine in this story? The wine is a symbol of the Holy Spirit! The Bible includes many references to this. For example, Ephesians 5:18 says, "And do not be drunk with wine, in which is dissipation; but be filled with the Spirit." Here the Bible refers to wine in comparison with the infillings of the Spirit. We also see in Job 32:18–19, "For I am full of words; the spirit within me compels me. Indeed my belly is like wine that has no vent; It is ready to burst like new wineskins." In these verses, both water (the word) and wine (the Spirit) are mentioned. Remember, the word always precedes the Spirit. So when you are filled with words as the waterpots were filled to the rim with water, the compelling of your spirit comes, like wineskins ready to burst. Your job is to be filled with the word, and then you will see that the compelling of the Spirit comes. If we continue reading, we find Job 32:21, which says, "Let me not, I pray, show partiality to anyone." You cannot show partiality. You are filled with the word, and now the Spirit moves over your life, your decisions, and everything else. The Spirit won't oblige you to do anything; He will simply compel you in your spirit. It is still your decision to make the move or not.

Once you are filled with the word and the Spirit, you will see major changes in your life. Even though you will be tempted, you will overcome. You will see that sin has lost its attraction for you. The power of the darkness will grow weaker as you step into the light. You will project righteousness, godly love, courage, and all of the Spirit's fruits. You will not longer have to strive for those things relying on your own effort. They will just become evident in your life, and you will walk in God's power. Wherever and whenever you go, you will be a mighty instrument of God. People will see the light of God shine in your life and come to Him because of you. You will have a supernatural ability to tackle any challenges you face. Your relationship with Jesus will be beyond what the mind can explain. You will understand the love of God the Father, the grace of our Lord Jesus, and the communion of the Holy Spirit. You will find fulfillment in God. Your life will stand for the glory of God: "That the name of our Lord Jesus Christ may be glorified in you, and you in Him" (2 Thessalonians 1:12). God knows those who glorify Him. People may not see you as God's instrument when you are still in the process of being shaped, but God knows all the potential that He put in you. Just wait until God says it is time for you to show yourself to the rest of the world. As He equips you in your time alone with the word, He will set you high up on the mountain so others will see His light shining through you. As you obey Him continually, you will see yourself growing more. God will entrust you with bigger responsibilities as you show Him that you are faithful. "And he said to him, 'Well done, good servant; because you were faithful in a very little, have authority over ten'" (Luke 19:17). That way you will live a life full of testimonies to the glory of God. At the end of your life's journey, others will say of you that you served according to the will of God and died leaving a legacy just like David. Acts 13:36 says, "For David, after he had served his generation by the will of God, fell asleep."

PART TWO

What Happens After You Are Filled with the Spirit?

Now that you are saturated with the word of God, you will start recognizing the movement of the Holy Spirit in your life. It's just like when the Spirit of God was hovering over the waters (word) in Genesis, the beginning. You will be an instrument for God to work through. You will be ready for God to work with you and everything that belongs to you. He works through you to shine His light upon others. Let's see some changes that will happen after you are filled with the Spirit, shall we?

8— You will find Him

The disciples said, "We found Him of whom Moses in the law, and also the prophets, wrote—Jesus of Nazareth, the son of Joseph" (John 1:45). Where did they find Him? In the scripture!

Who did they find? Jesus, the Word made flesh. Nathanael asked, "Can anything good come out of Nazareth?" and Philip replied, "Come and see." Nathanael went with Philip and met Jesus, and Jesus spoke to him. Nathanael instantly recognized Jesus as the Son of God, the king of Israel. Jesus replied, "You will see greater things than these." Indeed, that was just the beginning. Nathanael saw good and greater things after that. You too will see good and greater things accompany your life. That will happen to you after you find Jesus. What do we mean by *find Jesus*? As you spend time with the word of God, you will find out why you were born on this earth, who Jesus Christ really is, and what your true identity is in Christ. Then you will testify that God is good all the time and that you have found what you have been looking for, Jesus of Nazareth!

⚷ You will be filled with faith

"So then faith comes by hearing, and hearing by the word of God" (Romans 10:17). Hearing the word of God means spending time with it. When you start spending time with the word of God, your faith gets the opportunity to be built little by little. Have you ever spent time with an untrusting person? After some time, you become untrusting too. You are being influenced! It's one or the other—we either influence or get influenced. Jesus warned us, saying, "Be careful what you listen to!" (Mark 4:24). So what are you listening to? It's just not listening; it is what you listen to most of the time. All the people who have an amazing faith didn't just wake up one day and have it. It took a process of committing their time to the word of God. If they were weak, then they spent time with the word of God and became strong. If they thought they couldn't do it at some time in their lives, then they spent time with the word of God until they were more than able. If they felt defeated at every turn, then they saturated their lives with the word of God and became more than conquerors. In Hebrews chapter 11, we see all kinds of heroes in the hall of faith. Verse 6 says, "But without faith, it is impossible to please God." Do you want to please God? You have got to have faith! How do you get there? Hearing from the word of God. I assure you, as you spend time with the word of God, you will find yourself believing and moving mountains with your faith.

8— You will live by the word

"Man shall not live by bread alone, but by every word that proceeds from the mouth of God" (Matthew 4:4). Yes, earning money may sustain you physically, but what sustains you amid hopelessness and depression is the word of God. It comforts you when you despair. The Holy Spirit reminds you of the words that you kept inside your heart during your studies of the Bible. This is why some people who have a lot of money but no relationship with God die by suicide in their hours of despair. At times, some feel abandoned with no one to turn to. Money (bread) alone won't do you much good in such desperate times, but the word of God gives you wholesome security. It is the word that proceeds out of the mouth of God! You will go your way confident and secured. Proverbs 3:23–24 says, "Then you will walk safely in your way, and your foot will not stumble. When you lie down, you will not be afraid; yes, you will lie down and your sleep will be sweet." You will be safe physically, mentally, and spiritually. You will fear no evil even though you walk through dark valleys. Many people hear news reports and get disturbed about the future, globalization, their financial situations, and so forth. When you are filled with the word of God, your inside is calm. And when you are calm, you will hear God's voice pointing you to the solution. You will know what to do about any given situation. That will make your sleep sweet. Praise the Lord!

⚷— You will start recognizing the voice of the Lord

When you read the Bible, you will start recognizing the voice of the Lord. The word of God says in John 10:4, "And the sheep follow him, for they know his voice." The Bible represents Christians as sheep and Jesus as our shepherd. Jesus is the one who said that we, His sheep, hear His voice. Speaking of hearing a voice, there are at least three voices you can hear: the voice of the Lord, the voice of your mind, and the voice of the devil. So how do you know which voice you are hearing? Jesus said His sheep recognize His voice. How do you do that? The answer lies in the word of God. Hebrews 4:12 says, "For the word of God is living and powerful, and sharper than any two-edged sword, piercing even to the divisions of soul and spirit, and joints and marrow, and is a discerner of the thoughts and intents of the heart." Here, we see that the word separates and makes divisions between the soul (your mind, will, and emotions) and the spirit (heart). You see, the Holy Spirit communicates with you through your spirit. To hear His voice, you need to be filled with His word. Then the word will do the separating between your soul and spirit, which in turn enables you to determine whether the voice that you are hearing is from the Lord or your mind, which processes its information from the outside world through your five senses. The word is sharper than a two-edged sword, and that's why it separates the spirit and the soul. The word is no ordinary sword; if it were, it wouldn't be able to cut something that is not solid. Any sword can cut through something solid or tangible, but only the word of God can cut between and separate what is of the spirit and what is of the soul, which is intangible by nature. You get it! Your job is to be filled with the word. And the job of the word is to separate what is of the spirit from what is of the soul so you recognize the voice of the Lord. After you learn to do that, you won't have a hard time recognizing the devil's voice and will flee from it. It is not that hard to recognize. It always tells you to do the opposite of God's will or of what the word of God says.

⌐━⌐ Miracles and signs will follow you

Mark 16:20 says, "And they went out and preached everywhere, the Lord working with them and confirming the word through the accompanying signs." Are you seeking God's miracles that are told of in the book of Acts to manifest in your time and your generation? Well, you are on the right track. And yes, it can be done. Notice that the verse says "confirming the word through the accompanying signs"; this means that, when you are filled with the word and go out to preach, signs and miracles will follow you. Why? The miracles and signs are confirmations that God is alive now and forevermore. They just don't show up unless you honor the word. Through you, God can now reach out to the sick and the oppressed. Because here on this earth, we are His eyes, ears, and limbs. We are His body through which He can go places and do things. You will see His mighty hand upon you to perform signs and miracles in your life as well as deliver others from different forms of Satan's bondage. God does this to confirm to the world that he still lives and that what you are preaching about is His word. Through you, He will show the world that Jesus is the same yesterday, today, and forevermore.

⚷ You are cleansed and sanctified

Ephesians 5:26 says, "That He might sanctify and cleanse her with the washing of water by the word." Are you tired of sin defeating you? Do you feel like you need cleansing? Is there an area in your life that needs cleansing? Come to the word of God! He will cleanse and sanctify you. Jesus Himself said in John 17:17, "Sanctify them by your word. Your word is truth." The word has the power to sanctify you! How? As you give it your time and attention and meditate on it, it gains access to your innermost thoughts and intentions and changes your thinking. If your thinking is changed, you will no more be able to continue living in sin. You will thirst for the righteousness of God and begin hating sin so much that you will not engage in it. Your very nature changes when the word abides in you. So come to the word; it is waiting to cleanse and sanctify you so you can stand boldly in the presence of the Lord. "Now to Him who can keep you from stumbling, and to present you faultless before the presence of His glory with exceeding joy" (Jude 1:24).

8—⚷ You will be healed and delivered.

Psalm 107:20 says, "He sent His word and healed them, and delivered them from their destruction." The word delivers you from your fears, too. It delivers you from anxiety, stress, danger, and a lot more. You name it! The word of God will deliver you from destructive behavior. Matthew 8:8 says, "But only speak the word, and my servant will be healed." As long as you have the word, you can be healed. This is true! I experienced it and have told others that they can be healed too. In my Christian journey over the years, I have seen and heard so many testimonies of people being healed after they seriously commit themselves to the word of God, regardless of what sickness they had and what stage it had reached. I suffered from acute migraines for many years, even since I was a child. I tried medicines from within the country and even from England and the US. After accepting Christ, I prayed earnestly for God to take it away. Nothing happened! It was so severe that, by the time I was in high school, I would go out of the class, run to the washroom to throw up, and then ask permission to leave so I could go home to rest. That became my daily routine. I also tried going to every conference held, and when they announced that they were going to pray for the sick, I would go out and be prayed for, but still nothing happened! As the years went by, I felt hopeless, accepted the migraines as mine, and stopped praying about them. I stopped going to healing conferences too, but I couldn't stop wondering why God hadn't heal me at any of those times. But then, six years after accepting Christ as my Savior, I was fed up with how I, a born-again Christian, didn't understand the word. You see, I never was seriously committed to the word for all those years. Of course, I was reading the Bible, but it was not consistent. Sometimes a month would go by without my reading it. I was going to church, prayer meetings, and every other activity but never commit personal time to it. And nobody told me that I had to. So naturally, I couldn't understand what the Bible taught other than salvation. Then, at one point in 2004, I became so frustrated with not fully knowing what I held dear and important to me, life in Christ, that I decided I should seriously commit to read the Bible because it is the only source that could show me what I was seeking. I knelt before the Lord and said, "Okay, Lord! I know you exist, and I know you have saved me through Jesus from eternal damnation. But that cannot be all of it. I want to know how to live fully before I come to join you in heaven. Now I am having a lot of trouble understanding your ways; the way I am hearing about you from others is so confusing to me. Some of it seems not justified even. I don't believe you are that God. I want to know you. I want to understand your word; I want to know how to pray to you without so much effort. I am here before you to make an oath to you that I will give an hour every day to read your word, and you reveal your word to me. Help me, and thank you." The next day, I started reading the Bible. I read for an hour every day for three months—not that I stopped reading then, but it was after three months that I started realizing that the changes I was seeking were happening in my life. First of all, the words of God became easier for me to understand; I got revelations upon revelations. Second, I found out who God is and what His stand is in so many of life's issues and found Him to be rightly just. Third, I was healed, even though I never prayed for healing during that time. The sickness was just lifted away from me. I never changed anything in my eating habits or daily activities; I didn't change any of what I was doing already. This happened because of the power of God in His word. And I never had any problems with migraines after that. I have been sharing this with so many people over the years, and I have seen them getting healed as well. All they had to do was give time to the word of God. God healed them in their own houses! The word of God doesn't heal you only physically; it also heals your broken heart, your mind, and your broken relationships. This is true in every situation, and it applies to everyone. It's yours if you will take it!

⚷⊸ You will become a minister of the word.

You don't become a minister of the word just because you have spent many years as a Christian. The word of God says in Hosea 4:6, "Because you have rejected knowledge, I will also reject you from being a priest for me." If you don't spend time searching and understanding the word of God, you won't be able to represent

God. You could minister of your own will, but you won't see God's touch in your ministry, nor will He give you revelation or recognize your ministry. Representing God is what it means to be a priest or minister. On the other hand, if you give time to His word and do not reject His knowledge, you will become His priest. He will reveal His words to you, equip you with knowledge and power, and send you where you never thought you could be. That's what happened to me as I spent time with His word. I found answers to so many of my questions. I started sharing the word of God with others. Many of them told me that I gave them a message that spoke to their current situations. I became a blessing to others too. As time passed, I found out that I had become a minister of the word. I never thought I would teach the word and train others too. Apostle Peter said this once in Acts 10:34: "In truth, I perceive that God shows no partiality. But in every nation whoever fears Him and works righteousness is accepted." This is for anyone who seeks the Lord and wants to do His will. Praise God! Ever since then, I have enjoyed my Christian life, and I wouldn't want anything else. You can have that life too! When God equips you, nothing stands in your way. God will make a way for you because you are carrying His word. Whoever you are and whatever obstacles come your way, He will hold your hand and break open the doors that are holding you back.

8 — Your life will have form and purpose.

The word of God says in Genesis 1:2, "And the earth was without form and void, and darkness was upon the face of the deep." And then what happened? "And God said, 'Let there be light,' and there was light" (Genesis 1:3). If you feel like you are walking in darkness, feeling empty, and nothing makes sense in your life, then when you are filled with the word of God—the waters—the Spirit will move over your life to give it light and form. The light will show you what is happening and drive out the darkness that's been surrounding you. Where the light is, darkness flees away! And just as He gave the earth form, He will give you purpose. He made the earth conducive for living for the many generations that were to come. The earth has a purpose! It was made to sustain us for generations. And you will find out what God has intended for you to do in your lifetime. You will know your life's purpose and pursue it with God's strength. When you find your purpose, you will be full of light and form.

⚷ You will know how to pray.

I will give you a little testimony of how my prayer life was and how the word of God taught me to pray. The hardest thing for me to do was pray. I knew the Lord's Prayer ("Our father who art in heaven ...) by heart. I recited it morning, noon, and night when I was a kid because that was how my mom raised my siblings and me. We would recite it before every meal and before we slept. After we finished, we would add three requests: for God to give our parents a long life, to enlighten our minds so we would do well in school, and for our hair to grow long. It's silly, but God did grant us all three requests. God listens to our prayers, no matter how silly or childish they may seem. Praise be to Him. I will tell you, though, that my siblings and I treated prayer as a racing competition. We competed with one another to see who could recite it faster. We were only kids. After we grew up and accepted Christ as our Savior and Lord, my sister and I were taught some basic faith lessons. Then we joined the prayer team. Going to prayer meetings was stressful because the people there prayed for two straight hours. We had never prayed for more than five minutes in our lives. We wondered what they could be praying about for two whole hours. I struggled a great deal in prayer, so I did everything I could to avoid going to that prayer meeting. But I didn't stop there! I began searching for knowledge about it. Finally, I understood why people would pray for hours because I started doing it too! I also found out that it was really easy. How did I get there? Through the word of God! At first, I started reading the book of Psalm. I would kneel on the floor, put the Bible on the bed, open it up, and start reading from chapter 1 up until I found a word that spoke to my heart—you know, the one that I felt like my soul was trying to say but wasn't able to figure out how to say it. Since the book of Psalm contains songs and poems, I found it to be very expressive to what my soul was yearning for. I said it again and again prayerfully. I started from chapter 1 so that, the next day when I came to pray, I could remember where I had left off. I still do this today, and I think about what I read in the scripture. I think about how it applies to my life, and then I bring it up in the presence of God. Prayer is chatting with someone who is always interested in listening to what you have to say and communicating with you. There is nothing more personal than prayer. You can talk to God about what you think regarding what you have read in the Bible. You can ask Him if you have questions about it, and He will direct you to other verses or a story from the Bible that will give you more insight on the subject. Remember, one job of the Holy Spirit is to remind you and lead you to the truth. The Holy Spirit can really guide you the way you can understand it, but if you think you are not yet ready to hear Him, He will use other means to teach you. He will let you hear it either from a sermon or from someone else teaching about the subject. When you come to pray, tell Him how your day was and how you feel about it. Ask Him to give you wisdom on how to handle things. The benefits of prayer are endless, but we do need to learn how to pray according to His word. James 4:2–3 says, "Yet you do not have because you do not ask. You ask and do not receive, because you ask amiss, that you may spend it on your pleasures." His word sheds some light on why we do not receive answers when we ask in prayer. The first point is that we don't ask, so ask! Second, knowing God's nature and His being the one to grant you your desires, you can't expect Him to grant you evil things. He is good even to those who don't know Him and don't want Him. That is why you must be filled with His word so you understand how God works. God is good by nature, and He has made us partakers of that nature through Jesus Christ our Lord. That is why we need to understand His words well. When you understand what the Bible is about, you don't need to read psalms so you can pray. When you are filled with the word, God will reveal His will to you. When you read the Bible prayerfully and try to get closer to God, you will not be alone. He will already be there! His word in 2 Timothy 3:16 says, "All Scripture is God-breathed." The Holy Spirit is the author of the Bible! When you are open to reading the Bible with an honest desire, He will personally teach you so many things. Prayer is one of them. He is the Spirit in the word. You will learn to grow day by day. You may start little, but you will definitely grow. Soon you will be able to pray as much as you desire.

8 ⚷ You will know how to fight your battles.

Psalm 144:1 says, "Blessed be the Lord my rock, who trains my hands for war, and my fingers for battle." The world we live in is full of challenges. Everybody fights to live, to be stress-free, to be happy, to be successful, and to have more. As a Christian, you have the devil as your enemy, but he is a defeated foe. Christ has already won for you. But you still need to fight your battles. Christians are warriors; the Bible refers to us as soldiers. Soldiers fight! How do you do that? David says that the Lord taught him how to fight. Yes, the Lord will train you how to fight any and every battle you face and win. The word of God says in Paul's epistle to the Ephesians that our battle is not with flesh but with Satan and his demons in the heavens. Who do you fight against? Satan and his demons. Where is the fight? In the heavens. What weapons and armor do you need to wear? The helmet of salvation; the sword of the Spirit, which is the word of God; the shield of faith; the breastplate of righteousness; the belt of truth; and the shoes of the gospel of peace. That's how the Lord teaches you, through His word. You are not to just beat around the bush; it is a battle in which you must know where to aim. Before you go out to the battle, you need to know! Notice the key words in the description of the armor: salvation, righteousness, truth, faith, word of God, and gospel of peace. That's where the word of God comes in handy. It will teach you what power these words have to transform you and enable you to withstand the evil days. As for training, as you learn the word and take it with you, acting on it, you will become an experienced warrior over time. You are already an overcomer because of what Jesus did for you on the cross. Now go and conquer your fears, doubts, luck, and every challenge you have!

PART THREE

Where to Start and Grow

You might be thinking, *Now I get it. All I have to do is read the word of God. But where do I start—the Old Testament or the New Testament?* Here are some tried and proven tips to help you get a fresh start.

☛ Read the Bible

Read the Bible like any other book. Many people hesitate to read the word of God because of the high level of respect they have for it. They think that, if they read it by themselves, they will get judged. This is a problem because the Bible is there to direct us to the one who will make us whole. The Bible is not there to judge us. God knows we can't do anything apart from Him. It's why He wants us to get close to Him. So we know He is the one who will strengthen us to walk the righteous path. He didn't give us the Bible just to make us feel judged every time we see ourselves fail. He gave us His word so we can know who He is and how He works. And the only way to do that is to start reading the Bible. In His word, we will see that He is for us and not against us. Some believe that people can't just read the Bible by themselves. They say that it is very dangerous for laypeople to read the Bible by themselves because they may misinterpret it. They believe people should read other religious texts and go through rigorous discipline and years of Bible school before they read the Bible. Also, a lot of people are scared to read the Bible. Some try to read by just opening it up to any random page. Suppose they open to the book of Isaiah the first time they dare to read it. They may think that they have made a horrible mistake. I have heard of some people even repenting for daring to read it by themselves. Listen, God didn't inspire people to translate the Bible into so many languages just to reserve it for the eyes of few priests. I love the ministry of Jesus because He came bearing all the Old Testament laws and prophets and taught them in simple, laypeople's terms. Jesus's ministry was good news to *all,* not just to the privileged few, the scholarly, the priests, or the poor. It is for everyone who wants to know! So go get your Bible and read it by yourself. You can start with the first page. The book of Genesis tells stories about how everything began. It's not something you will forget after reading because it has interesting stories that are so captivating that they won't simply leave your mind. Yes, some people can't remember what they have read as soon as they finish reading. It's because they are trying to read from the teachings. Those are not hard to grasp. As I stated earlier, the Bible is written for just any layperson who can read. But the Bible contains texts of different categories: some are stories, some are teachings, some are prophecies, some are songs and poems, and some are just history. So if you are a beginner, start reading the stories. Why? Our brains are wired that way. We can't forget stories! We have been told many stories since we were little. It doesn't take much for us to remember and narrate them, right? Some of us could even dramatize them. So there you have it! Your first challenge is done. Start reading!

How much is enough though? Many people ask this. It depends on you. If you are already in the habit of reading, you can read as much as you want. At times, I have read the whole book of Genesis in one day. I read one book a day when I want to saturate my mind with the word of God. How do I do that? I read as fast as I can. Some could argue that reading quickly could lead to missing many things, but the opposite is true. Research shows that, when you read faster, you are commanding the full and undivided attention of your mind. Your mind is so occupied with what's at hand that you can remember much of what you read. Is it guaranteed that you will remember every word? No. But that's a sure way to remember most of it. If you are not a good reader, no problem! You can start with just a chapter. Some chapters are not even one page long. Or you can set a timer for yourself, say, ten to fifteen minutes daily. Once you start reading the Bible, it will take you further than you had planned. Trust me, it is that good. Try it!

Also, read the Bible like no other book. After you have read most of it quickly and can remember most of it, start reading it slowly. By *slowly*, I mean take the time to understand the lesson in each story. You can read a story, a chapter, or a verse. You will need to find a quiet time and place when you are not constantly distracted. It must not be when you are busy doing other things. Find a quiet time that is convenient for you. For some people, it is the evening; some prefer early in the morning before others in the house are up; for some, it is during the day when everyone else is gone to work or school; and for others, it is when everyone is taking a nap in the afternoon. So choose a quiet time when you are most comfortable and can give your undivided attention. Now, when you read, start by saying a little prayer. Pray that God reveals His word for you and opens your eyes so you see Him in the scriptures. Make it personal! Tell Him how much it means to you. Then start reading.

You can choose a passage to read by yourself. It could be a verse, a couple of verses, a chapter, or a few chapters. As you read, try finding the lessons you can get from it. When you find a word that speaks to your life or situation, read it over and over again. Compare it with what is going on in your life. If what you are passing through is different from what the word of God says, then take the word of God and claim it over your life or situation. If you think things must change, then change them. Our thoughts and traditions usually hinder us from becoming what the word of God says about us. For example, if you think that you are under a curse while being a Christian, then you are wrong because Christ took your curse away at the cross! He became a curse so that you could become blessed of the Lord. No need for you to keep on paying your debts. Jesus paid it all in full!

Imagine what happens the day you learn this truth from the word of God: your life changes for the better! Why? Proverbs

23:7 says, "As a man thinks, so he is." If your thinking is changed, your whole living will be changed. When your thinking falls in line with the word of God, you will see changes. That is why we must spend time with the word of God and learn what it says about us, our situations, and others. You are a child of God, and you have certain privileges as a result. You also have the authority to break or mend things. You are a new creation in Christ! You have a new heavenly identity. That new identity is what gives you access to God's blessings over your life. The word is a mighty instrument in your hand; use it! The word is Spirit-breathed; that's why it comes to life when you read it. And when you think and live as the word says, you will bring dead things to life. As you read, the Holy Spirit will guide you in simple ways that you can understand. For example, you may feel inclined to read one verse again and again, or you may look at it in ways you have never thought you could. Rest assured, it is the Holy Spirit guiding you to focus on that script specifically. At times like that, hang in there; don't hurry yourself to finish what you planned to read for the day. The Holy Spirit is highlighting that specific text for you because that's what He is trying to tell you right at that moment. That's one way the Lord guides you. As you go back to read the scripture, sometimes you will notice that your mind also brings up similar verses or stories and tries to connect them to your current situation. That is also the Holy Spirit showing you in a broader sense what He wants you to understand.

At that moment, go to the verses or chapters that you are reminded of and read them. If you'll notice, all the verses and stories you are guided to have the same message. You will see a repetitive message in all of them. And that, my friend, is the Holy Spirit talking to you. There is your answer! Search for it as if you are hunting for a hidden treasure. Don't stop until you find the answer to your question. If you do this, you will find the Lord and understand what the scriptures are about. Proverbs 2:1 and 5 say, "My son, if you receive my words and treasure my commands within you … then you will understand the fear of the Lord, and find the knowledge of God."

⚷ Meditate

Now that you know how to read the Bible and how to be led by the Holy Spirit through His word, you need to keep His word in your heart. One way to do that is to meditate. That is the key! There's a saying that goes, "An idle mind is the devil's workshop." You can't keep your mind empty and expect change. If you give time and read the word, you will understand what the Lord is saying to you. But when you get up and forget all of it to go about your daily life, then you cannot have a victorious life. You are only halfway through! You need to take to heart what you learned in your quiet time so that the word can take root in your life. Meditation will help with that. What do I mean by *meditation*? It just means that you think about the word over and over. Meditation is not about having many thoughts or no thoughts at all and wandering here and there without purpose. Meditation is guided thinking through the word of God.

The Bible says, "This book of the Law shall not depart from

your mouth, but you shall meditate on it day and night, that you may observe to do according to all that is written in it. For then you will go your way prosperous, and then you will have success" (Joshua 1:8). Let's break down this verse bit by bit. First of all, we meditate on the word of God; *the Law* means "the word of God." Read it first and then memorize it. Always start with a verse that you like, just one verse per week. Memorize the verse and say it over and over during the week. Think about what it means and how it can apply to your life or current situation. *Second*, meditate on it day and night. What does this mean? Meditate on it when you are walking, waiting for the bus or somebody else, and when you are praying. As you continue doing one verse per week, train yourself to memorize even harder verses. To help you memorize the harder or longer verses, try associating them with something familiar to you, something to remind you of your day-to-day life. Do this until the verse sticks to you and you are a natural at it. It is not a must that you meditate on a new verse each week. If it is not sticking to you, give it more time. You will find out that memorizing and meditating on verses will come in handy in times of need. There is no way you will become a powerful Christian without the habit of meditating. In the Bible, we can name David and Joshua as people who meditated. Meditation gives you enough time and ground for God's plans to be conceived in your spirit to bring them to fruition. You have God's promises spoken over your life; meditation is the most conducive environment to bring them to fruition. It is the fertile land you prepare before you sow your seed. Meditation on the word of God prepares and transforms your mind to be in line with your spirit. The Bible in Romans 12:2 says, "And do not be conformed to this world, but be transformed by the renewing of your mind, that you may prove what is that good and acceptable and perfect will of God." When you meditate, your mind is transformed, and then you are able to do the will of God. Meditation helps you focus on what the Lord says about your life. And when you devote time and much thought to His promises, whatever you do will prosper. The Bible says that Joseph prospered because God was with Him (Genesis 39:2). When you meditate on the word, God will bless everything you do. Read Joshua 1:8 again: "This book of law shall not depart from your mouth, but you shall meditate in it day and night, that you may observe to do according all that is written in it. For then you will have good success." See? When you put the word in your heart, it will have the opportunity to work in every area of your life and cause it to prosper.

⚷ Obey

After meditation comes obedience. What good is it to understand the scriptures and know what you must do if you don't act on that understanding? Live according to His word. If His word says something is wrong, consider it wrong. It is as simple as that. Your obedience starts with the way you think. You can research it and take time to understand it more before you simply accept it, but after you have found what you need to convince yourself that the action or thought is wrong, then make your decision and live your life in light of that. You need to align yourself with the word of God and then do it. Jesus said in Luke 6:46, "But why do you call Me 'Lord, Lord,' and do not do the things which I say?" When the Lord reveals His word to you, it's not just for the sake of knowledge. He shows you so you will change your thinking and your ways. And that is not a one-time change; it is a gradual change that takes a lifetime. Old habits die hard! You must keep changing into His likeness. When you obey one thing at a time, you are building yourself to be a useful instrument worthy of the manifestation of His glory. When you obey Him, He will reveal Himself to you. John 14:21 says, "He who has My commandments and keeps them, it is he who loves Me. And he who loves Me will be loved by My father, and I will love him and manifest Myself to him." Jesus manifests Himself only for those who obey His commandments. If God reveals something to you and you keep ignoring it, He won't reveal more to you. But if you act on it and walk toward it in faith, Jesus will manifest Himself to you not once or twice but every time!

8— Have consistency.

Whatever you do, do it consistently because doing so goes the longest of miles. It pays off well! You have heard the fable of the hare and the tortoise. It is not how fast you can run but whether you can reach the destination. The Christian walk is a lifelong commitment—no need for a rush. What is needed is for you to walk in the light of the word and grow consistently into the likeness of Christ. Growing by itself requires consistency. Suppose you have a plant. If it doesn't get sunshine, water, and fertile soil consistently, it won't grow. It will wither by the day and eventually die. Just like the plant, all Christians need to seek God consistently. Just like the branch of a tree takes nutrients consistently from the stem, we are to continually seek God through His word. Sometimes we read the Bible for a whole day and then don't read it for another three months. Listen! The key is to read every day no matter how little. It is better to read for ten minutes every single day than to read a large amount at once and then not read for a whole week. Why? Because you are building little by little, and that, my friend, will take you far in your life with Christ.

How important is consistency to my victorious Christian life? you may ask. Well, there are many instances where the word of God shows us the value of doing something consistently and how far it will take us. One instance is in the book of Kings. The story is recorded in 2 Kings 13, and in verses 14–21, we read that Joash, the king of Israel, came down to visit as the prophet Elisha was dying. The prophet told Joash to grab a bow and an arrow and to shoot the ground. The king shot three times and stopped. The prophet became furious and told the king that if he had shot five or six times, he would have won over his enemies till he destroyed them. But because he shot only three times, he was going to win only three times. Now, what do we learn from this story? We learn that we need to press on until God says otherwise. Prophets are God's mouthpiece. They represent God. What true prophets say comes to pass because they heard it from God. We need to be consistent when we ask God anything. We need to press on until He gives us what we want or until He says otherwise. Either way, we need to continue seeking Him through His word until He reveals himself to us.

Another example we have is the apostle Paul. He writes in 2 Corinthians 12:8– 9, "Concerning this thing I pleaded with the Lord three times that it might depart from me. And He said to me, 'My grace is sufficient for you, My strength is made perfect in weakness.'" Why did Paul ask only three times? We saw in the previous story in the book of Kings that the king shot three times, but the prophet of God told him it was no good. But here we see Paul saying that he prayed three times and got an answer. The key is not in how many times you pray; the key is how consistently you seek what you desire until you get your answer. Paul prayed until he got an answer. Press on until you get a breakthrough and get your answers.

8 Seek with all your heart

Nothing attracts God's attention as much as your seeking Him wholeheartedly! If you want to know more about God and His ways, you have to thirst for it. You must seek it with all your heart. Giving your heart halfway won't do. Seek it with all your heart, all your soul, and all your being. What does that mean? Give Him your time, give Him your utmost attention, obey Him, search for Him in prayer and His word, pay the price, and make Him your priority. People say they thirst for God, and then they get lazy about it. If you are thirsting for God and you are not doing anything about it, you will only grow frustrated. If you want to change your life and be a useful instrument of God, give Him time and search for His ways in His word. Proverbs 2:1–5 says, "My son, receive my words, and treasure my commands within you, so that you incline your ear to wisdom, and apply your heart to understanding; Yes, if you cry out for discernment, and lift your voice for understanding, if you seek her as silver, and search for her as for hidden treasures; Then you will understand the fear of the Lord, and find the knowledge of God." You see, we want to have all the big things like wisdom, understanding, and knowledge in our lives. We can have all of these, but they all come at a price if we are willing to pay. What is the price? We must receive God's word and treasure it, incline our ears and hearts, and cry out and seek discernment as we would a hidden treasure. All these require our time, attention, and obedience.

8━━ Seek Him in time that He may be found.

"Seek the Lord while He may be found; call upon Him while He is near" (Isaiah 55:6). People think there is always a tomorrow, but we don't know if tomorrow will come for us. Our time is not in our hands. Nobody knows when they are going to die. That is why we must think of living and doing the things we must do today. The Bible puts a lot of emphasis on today, the present time. For example, when you heard the good news of our Lord, if you decided to say yes to it, then you were saved right at that moment. So now is the time of salvation; now is the time of commitment; now is the time of change. Don't wait till tomorrow! Do it when your soul is still urging you to seek God. Relationships are a two-way street. God is always committed to you; will you appreciate that and match it? If not, there will come a time when you won't feel the spirit compelling you anymore. You will go about your busy life and forget the things of God. You will forget to nourish your spirit! You will wake up one day, and then it will be too late. So call on Him today! Make the necessary commitment and changes today. No time is like the present.

Final Thoughts

God is so close to you, closer than your breath! He wants to fellowship with you. He wants you to know Him and His ways. He wants to see you grow and be a responsible and powerful witness to Him. He wants to manifest Himself through you and let His light shine through you. Come to His word! All of these are at your fingertips; you can access them anytime you want because you are a child of the Almighty God!

In 2 Peter 1:8 we read, "For if you possess these qualities in increasing measure, they will keep you from being ineffective and unproductive in your knowledge of our Lord Jesus Christ."

As you build your time with the Lord and follow Him according to His Word, you will see it is an ever-increasing journey that will build lasting Christian character in you and help you bear much fruit. As you give yourself fully to obeying the word, you will bear the fruit of the Holy Spirit. John 15:16 says, "I chose you and appointed you that you should go and bear fruit and that your fruit should remain, that whatever you ask my father in My name He may give you." These fruits that Jesus referred to will be evident in your life. And if these will keep increasing, your life, relationships, ministry, and anything you put your mind to will be effective and productive, just like the tree in Psalm 1, planted by the rivers of water that bring forth fruit in its season. Let me leave one assignment for you to further your studies. Read Psalm 1:1–3 and relate it to what we have been studying in this book. You will quickly see that each part of the word of God is linked to the others to direct us to one truth—the word shapes everything.

Remember that you have His word in your own hands. You have sufficient grace. You have the fellowship of believers surrounding you. You have the angels of God protecting and fighting for you. Most of all, you have the Holy Spirit with you, your ever-present companion.

Blessings!

> Then he said to me, "Write: 'Blessed *are* those who
> are called to the marriage supper of the Lamb!'"
> (Revelation 19:9)

Printed in the United States
by Baker & Taylor Publisher Services